GW00775911

Drama for Students, Volume 17

Project Editor: David Galens

Editorial: Anne Marie Hacht, Michelle Kazensky, Ira Mark Milne, Pam Revitzer, Kathy Sauer, Timothy J. Sisler, Jennifer Smith, Carol Ullmann

Research: Nicodemus Ford, Sarah Genik, Tamara Nott

Permissions: Lori Hines

Manufacturing: Stacy Melson

Imaging and Multimedia: Robert Duncan, Mary Grimes, Lezlie Light, Kelly A. Quin, Luke Rademacher

Product Design: Pamela A. E. Galbreath, Michael Logusz

© 2003 by Gale. Gale is an imprint of The Gale Group, Inc., a division of Cengage Learning Inc.

Gale and Design® and Cengage Learning™ are

trademarks used herein under license.

For more information, contact
The Gale Group, Inc.
27500 Drake Rd.
Farmington Hills, MI 48331-3535
Or you can visit our Internet site at
http://www.gale.com

ALL RIGHTS RESERVED
No part of this work covered by the copyright
hereon may be reproduced or used in any form or
by any means—graphic, electronic, or mechanical,
including photocopying, recording, taping, Web
distribution, or information storage retrieval
systems—without the written permission of the
publisher.

For permission to use material from this product,
submit your request via Web at http://www.gale-
edit.com/permissions, or you may download our
Permissions Request form and submit your request
by fax or mail to:

Permissions Department
The Gale Group, Inc.
27500 Drake Rd.
Farmington Hills, MI 48331-3535
Permissions Hotline: 248-699-8006 or 800-877-
4253, ext. 8006
Fax: 248-699-8074 or 800-762-4058

Since this page cannot legibly accommodate all
copyright notices, the acknowledgments constitute
an extension of the copyright notice.

While every effort has been made to ensure the reliability of the information presented in this publication, The Gale Group, Inc. does not guarantee the accuracy of the data contained herein. The Gale Group, Inc. accepts no payment for listing; and inclusion in the publication of any organization, agency, institution, publication, service, or individual does not imply endorsement of the editors or publisher. Errors brought to the attention of the publisher and verified to the satisfaction of the publisher will be corrected in future editions.

ISBN 0-7876-6032-9
ISSN 1094-9232

Printed in the United States of America
10 9 8 7 6 5 4 3 2 1

The Duchess of Malfi

John Webster 1623

Introduction

John Webster's *The Duchess of Malfi* was written in 1613 or 1614, and had at least two successful productions in London before it was published in 1623 under the title *The Tragedy of the Duchesse of Malfy*. Generally considered to be Webster's masterpiece, it tells the story of a young widow who marries against the wishes of her powerful brothers, setting off a storm of revenge. The startling violence, the unbelievable plot twists, the mysterious motives of the brothers, and the calm strength of the Duchess have made *The Duchess of*

Malfi a subject for fierce debate for hundreds of years. Critics and reviewers have loved or hated the play, with equal fervor.

The Duchess's story is based on actual events that took place in Italy in the early sixteenth century. Webster freely borrowed elements of his story from several sources, including William Painter's popular collection of stories, *The Palace of Pleasure* (1566–1567), and Sir Philip Sidney's romance *Arcadia* (1590), and also borrowed dramatic elements from the Revenge Tragedy tradition, but he adapted the source materials to suit his own themes and dramatic purpose. *The Duchess of Malfi* is widely available in high school and college anthologies. It is also available separately as a Dover Thrift edition and collected in *The Duchess of Malfi and Other Plays* (1998), part of the Oxford World Classics series.

Author Biography

John Webster was born in London, England, probably in 1579 or 1580. Like most of the facts about Webster's life, his birthdate is not recorded in any documents that survive to this day; scholars estimate his birthdate by extrapolating from existing records of his parents' marriage in 1577. It is known that his father was also named John and that the father earned a good living as a coachmaker, but the name and background of Webster's mother is not known.

It is likely that Webster attended the prestigious Merchant Taylors' School, an institution established for children of members of the Company of Merchant Taylors. There, he would have received a solid basic education, which included exposure to literature in Latin and English, and he would have participated in musical and dramatic performances.

Although the play itself has been lost, there is evidence that Webster was part of a group that was paid in 1602 for writing *Caesar's Fall*. This play, written on commission, is the earliest known work to which Webster contributed. Webster would continue to collaborate with other playwrights, including Thomas Dekker, Thomas Middleton, and Michael Drayton, for much of his career. Most of these plays were written for performance by particular theatrical companies. They were intended to be popular successes, not texts for study, and the successful playwright was able to produce histories, comedies, tragedies—whatever the market demanded. In or near 1605, Webster married a woman named Sara Peniall. Their first son, also named John, was baptized in 1606, and several other children followed. Webster was apparently able to support his family through his writing.

Webster's two most important plays were both written by him alone: *The White Devil* (1612) and *The Duchess of Malfi* (published 1623, but written in 1613 or 1614). Both draw heavily on the Italian tradition of sensation and tragedy, which was popular at the time. Webster also wrote prose "character" sketches, a ceremonial pageant, and various odes and verses, none of which is as important today as his plays. Over his career, Webster wrote approximately ten plays in collaboration and at least four individually. During his lifetime, he was well-known as a playwright and as a visible member of London's upper middle class.

Webster's last known play, *Appius and Virginia*, was produced in London in 1634. Though no records of his death have been found, references to Webster in the work of other writers seem to indicate that he died no later than late 1634.

Plot Summary

Act 1

    The Duchess of Malfi is divided into five acts, each comprising several scenes. In the three scenes of act 1, the major characters and conflicts are introduced. The setting is the Italian city of Amalfi in the sixteenth century, in the audience chamber or "presence" of the widowed Duchess. Antonio, the Duchess's steward, talks with his friend Delio as they observe the others who pass through the chamber. The first to enter are the Cardinal and Bosola. Although Bosola has recently been released after serving seven years for a murder he committed at the behest of the Cardinal, the Cardinal is cold to him and will not acknowledge his debt.

    Ferdinand, the Duke of Calabria, enters with his entourage. Ferdinand learns that Antonio has proven himself the best at a knightly competition, and he congratulates Antonio for his prowess and for his eloquent speech. When the Cardinal reenters with the Duchess, Antonio gives Delio his impression of the three siblings: the Cardinal is jealous and vengeful, Ferdinand is "perverse and turbulent," and the Duchess is sweet and noble. Ferdinand asks the Duchess to accept Bosola as a servant, and she agrees; in fact, the brothers have hired Bosola to spy on the Duchess.

    The two brothers warn the Duchess not to

remarry, and she promises that she will not. However, as soon as they leave her chamber, she summons Antonio and the two perform a private marriage ceremony, with the Duchess's trusted servant Cariola as witness.

Act 2

The second act, which has five scenes, begins several months later, as the Duchess is about to give birth to a child. Her marriage to Antonio is still secret, and she has concealed her pregnancy by wearing loose clothing. Bosola, however, suspects that she is pregnant and tries to trap her by giving her a present of apricots. When she devours them hungrily and then vomits, he has confirmation of the pregnancy but does not reveal what he knows. The incident sends the Duchess into labor, and she is rushed to her chamber.

To avoid suspicion that the Duchess is giving birth, a ruse is invented: it is announced that jewels have been stolen, and everyone must stay in his or her room while a search is conducted. The Duchess delivers a healthy son, and when Cariola tells Antonio the good news, he prepares a set of calculations based on astrology to determine the baby's future. Meanwhile, Bosola sneaks out to the courtyard beneath the Duchess's window and hears her crying out. Antonio finds him there, and they argue about Bosola having left his room. As he leaves Bosola, Antonio accidentally drops the paper on which he has written his astrological notes, and

Bosola retrieves it, discovering that a baby has been born to the Duchess—a baby who will have a short life. Bosola knows that Antonio is in on the secret but does not consider that a man of Antonio's social class could be the father.

In Rome, the Cardinal meets in his chamber with Julia, his mistress. Delio arrives and propositions Julia, but she refuses him. In another part of the Cardinal's palace, Ferdinand has received a letter from Bosola, telling him of the baby's birth. The Cardinal and Ferdinand discuss their sister's betrayal, and Ferdinand's rage takes him to the brink of insanity.

Act 3

Several years pass before the five scenes in act 3 take place. The Duchess has given birth to two more children, but her marriage is still a secret, and Bosola still has not discovered the identity of the father. Ferdinand, finally stirred to action, arrives at the Duchess's palace to confront her. To play an affectionate joke on her, Antonio and Cariola step out of the room while the Duchess is talking to herself in the mirror, and Ferdinand comes into the room at the same moment. He accuses her of shaming the family with her promiscuity, and although she tells him that she is married, he vows never to look at her again.

Afraid of Ferdinand's anger, the Duchess sends Antonio to safety by pretending that he has stolen money and been banished. Tenderly, the couple say goodbye to each other, planning to reunite in Ancona. In her grief, the Duchess confides in Bosola, telling him everything. Bosola plots to entrap the Duchess and Antonio. He speeds to Rome to tell what he knows and find his reward, and the brothers respond with expected fury. The Cardinal decides to contact the authorities at Ancona and have the Duchess and her family banished.

At the Shrine of Our Lady of Loretto, the Duchess and Antonio review their situation. Bosola brings a letter from Ferdinand calling for Antonio's death, and Antonio and the Duchess say goodbye again. They know that this will be their final parting. Antonio takes their oldest son and flees to Milan. The Duchess is arrested by Bosola, in disguise, and taken by guards to her palace.

Act 4

Act 4, with its two scenes set in the Duchess's chambers, moves quickly. Trying to drive her to despair so that she will be damned as well as killed, Ferdinand arranges for a series of horrors. He visits the Duchess in a darkened room (because he has vowed never to see her again) and places in her hand a dead man's hand that she will assume to be Antonio's. He shows her wax figures that look like the bodies of Antonio and the three children. He arranges for eight madmen to scream outside her window. Through it all, the Duchess maintains her quiet nobility, saying "I am Duchess of Malfi still," and Bosola begins to feel a grudging respect for her.

Finally, Bosola brings two executioners to the Duchess's chamber, and they strangle her. She faces her death with dignity. Cariola is also strangled, though she resists her death with all her energy. Off stage, the two younger children are strangled. When Ferdinand sees his dead sister, he has a dramatic change of heart, and rather than rewarding Bosola, he blames him for the murders.

Act 5

The action of the five scenes of act 5 is also rapid. Four days after the events in act 4, the Cardinal has had all of Antonio's property seized. Antonio decides to visit the Cardinal and attempt a reconciliation. Ferdinand's madness has increased, and he has been seen digging up bodies in the cemetery and carrying a man's leg over his shoulder. Bosola arrives in Milan, and he and the Cardinal try to determine what the other knows. The Cardinal pretends that he does not know the Duchess is dead, so that he will not seem to have been involved in the murder, but Bosola persuades Julia to find out the truth. The Cardinal confesses to Julia that he has had his sister killed, but then he immediately kills Julia with a poisoned book.

Outside the Cardinal's home, Antonio and Delio speak with a ghostly echo that comes from the Duchess's grave. Bosola vows to protect Antonio from harm, but he accidentally kills Antonio with his sword, mistaking him for the Cardinal, who has promised to kill Bosola. In the final scene, an anguished Bosola kills the Cardinal's servant and stabs the Cardinal. Ferdinand rushes in and stabs Bosola and the Cardinal. Bosola stabs Ferdinand. As they all lie dead, Delio enters with Antonio's son and calls for a unified effort to support the young man as the new Duke.

Characters

Antonio Bologna

Antonio is the steward, or the manager, of the Duchess of Malfi's palace. He is good with a horse and a lance, and he is widely known to be honest— so honest that the Cardinal rejects a suggestion that Antonio be hired to spy on the Duchess. He is also a good judge of character, delivering to his friend, Delio, insightful descriptions of the others as they appear. He is in awe of the Duchess, because of her beauty and her disposition, and humbly accepts her proposal of marriage without regard for the wealth he will obtain by marrying her. In fact, he agrees to keep the marriage secret, and so he gains no power or prestige from it. After he is married, Antonio is less sharply drawn, but the glimpses given of him do not fulfill the promise of act 1. He loses the paper on which he has calculated the baby's future. He follows the Duchess's plans for avoiding capture, making no suggestions himself. Finally, he is killed as he walks to the Cardinal's door to ask for a reconciliation. Still, he is a good man, and the Duchess clearly loves and trusts him until the end.

Media Adaptations

- *The Duchess of Malfi* was produced for television in 1972 by the BBC. The 123-minute VHS cassette, featuring performances by Eileen Atkins, Michael Bryant, and Gary Bond, is distributed by Time-Life Video.

- The BBC produced an audio recording of the play in 1980, starring Dame Peggy Ashcroft and Paul Scolfield. This production runs on three audiocassettes, and is distributed by Audio-Forum.

- An older audio version originally issued on record albums, but since 1972 distributed on three audiocassettes, is also available from Caedmon. It features Barbara Jefford as the Duchess, and includes a booklet with biographical information and essays on the play.

- In 1962, Caedmon issued a recording of excerpts from the play read by the British poet Dylan Thomas, well known for his wonderful speaking voice. The recording is available from Caedmon on one audiocassette.

Daniel de Bosola

Bosola is the Duchess's Provisor of Horse. As the play opens, he has just been released from imprisonment because of "a notorious murder" the Cardinal hired him to commit. Now, he is employed by Ferdinand, who arranges his position with the Duchess so he can spy on her and prevent her from marrying. In many ways, Bosola is the most complex character in the play, and the only one whose thinking and personality change from beginning to end. Antonio predicts this change at the beginning, when he comments that Bosola is "very valiant," but worries that his melancholy will "poison all his goodness." In fact, Bosola is capable of great evil. He spies on the Duchess (though he is unable in three years to discover that Antonio is the Duchess's husband), supervises her murder and the murder of her children and of Cariola, accidentally kills Antonio, and deliberately kills the Cardinal,

Ferdinand, and a servant. As he observes the nobility of the Duchess and Antonio in facing death and also sees that committing heinous acts for the Cardinal and Ferdinand does not win him gratitude or financial reward, he begins to question his belief that it is better "To appear a true servant, than an honest man." But, when the "stars" drive Bosola to kill Antonio, whom he has resolved to protect, he concludes that all human endeavor and human goodness are meaningless.

The Cardinal

The Cardinal is the brother of the Duchess and Ferdinand, as cold and calculating as Ferdinand is excitable. He is a high-ranking official in the Roman Catholic Church, but he does not live the life of a Christian saint: he has a mistress; he hires spies and murderers; and, he does not seem to have any religious duties or religious thought. As Antonio explains to Delio, "where he is jealous of any man, he lays worse plots for them than ever was imposed on Hercules, for he strews in his way flatterers, panders, intelligencers, atheists, and a thousand such political monsters."

The Cardinal is the quiet force behind the plotting against the Duchess. It is his idea to hire Bosola to spy on her, but even Bosola does not know of the Cardinal's involvement. When Bosola has killed the Duchess, the Cardinal pretends to have no knowledge of the crime. He shares Ferdinand's desire that the Duchess not marry, and

Ferdinand's anger when she bears a child, but he "can be angry *Without this rupture*" of "*intemperate noise.*" *He demonstrates no love or loyalty, treating with startling coldness Bosola, who killed and was punished in his employment, and Julia, who is his mistress, and the Duchess and Ferdinand, who are his siblings. His motives for tormenting his sister are not clear. He does not want her money or her love, and he is incapable of feeling humiliation or shame. He does not care for his reputation or legacy; his final words are "now, I pray, let me* Be laid by, and never thought of."

Cariola

Cariola is the trustworthy servant of the Duchess, privy to all of the Duchess's secrets. Cariola witnesses the marriage between the Duchess and Antonio, helps deliver the Duchess's children, and is with the Duchess when the Duchess dies. In her own death, she is not as noble as the Duchess, but kicks and screams and tries to escape. Throughout the play, she is more cautious than the Duchess, thinking that marrying Antonio is "madness," and fearing that the trick of a false pilgrimage will prove unlucky.

Delio

Delio is a courtier and a friend of Antonio. His main role in the story is to provide a sounding board for Antonio. Delio's curiosity about the court gives Antonio the opportunity to speak aloud about the characters of the Duchess, her brothers, and Bosola in the way an omniscient narrator might in a novel. Delio is also the friend in whom Antonio confides the secrets of his marriage and the births of his children; like Cariola, Delio guards the secrets carefully. Delio has no direct connection with any of the siblings, and he does not directly participate in their plots and deaths. He is the faithful friend, always standing by to help Antonio when he is needed. In a scene in act 2, Delio comes to Rome and makes advances to Julia, who rebuffs him. Their interaction affects nothing else in the play, and the two never meet again. Delio speaks the last words in the play, when he enters "too late" with Antonio's oldest son after his parents have been killed. He urges the survivors to help the young man gain his inheritance and proclaims, "Integrity of life is fame's best friend, / Which nobly, beyond death, shall crown the end."

The Duchess of Malfi

The Duchess of Malfi is the sister of the Cardinal and the twin sister of Ferdinand. She is never referred to by name throughout the play, but only by the labels that describe her roles as sister, duchess, and wife. As the play opens, she is a widow, but still in the bloom of youth. (According to Webster's source materials, the real duchess was a girl of twelve years old when she was married to a much older man; she became a widow when she was twenty.) Although her brothers forbid her to marry again, and she promises to obey them, she longs for a husband. Secretly, she asks her steward Antonio to marry her, and they perform a private marriage ceremony. Afraid of her brothers' anger, the Duchess manages to keep her marriage a secret for years, even through the birth of three children. When the brothers do learn of the children, she flees with Antonio but is captured and murdered.

Early in the play, Antonio describes her as a woman whose speech is "full of rapture," who has a "sweet countenance," who lives a life of "noble virtue." Although her sweet nobility casts no spell over her brothers, her every word and action support Antonio's judgment of her, and her subjects love and respect her. She is clever, able to match her brothers' wit in her exchanges with them, and able to quickly craft intricate plots for escape. She is affectionate with her husband, children, and servant, showing a tenderness that is far beyond the capabilities of the Cardinal and Ferdinand. And she is dignified in the face of her brothers' torments, stating even at the worst of it, "I am Duchess of Malfi still."

Some critics have commented that the Duchess deserves death because of her rashness in marrying beneath her station, but most reject that notion, agreeing that there is nothing in the play to indicate that Webster found fault with the marriage of Antonio and the Duchess. What happens to her is not her fault, but the result of living in a "gloomy world."

Ferdinand

Ferdinand, the Duke of Calbria, is the twin brother of the Duchess, younger than her by a few minutes. He is as emotional as his brother the Cardinal is icy, and his response to the idea of his sister marrying is beyond all bounds. Ferdinand's motivation has always been a central question for critics of this play, and many critics have seen incestuous feelings in his rage. Whatever the cause, when he learns that his sister has given birth to a child, he declares her a whore and "a sister damn'd," creates a mental picture of her "in the shameful act of sin," and imagines burning her and her lover in a coal pit with no vent, so that "their curs'd smoke might not ascend to heaven," or boiling her child into a soup and serving it to the father.

As with other characters, Antonio's early description of Ferdinand proves insightful. Antonio tells Delio that Ferdinand has "a most perverse, and turbulent nature." Even the Cardinal wonders whether Ferdinand is "stark mad," and after brooding over his sister's betrayal for a time, Ferdinand does approach insanity. After he has had the Duchess killed and sees her lying dead, he regrets that he ordered Bosola, "when I was distracted of my wits, / Go kill my dearest friend," but there has been no hint previously that he and the Duchess shared any closeness.

The realization of what he has done pushes Ferdinand over the edge into insanity, perhaps even to the point of imagining that he is a werewolf. He is found in the graveyard digging up dead bodies and is seen "with the leg of a man *Upon his shoulder; and he howl'd fearfull,* Said he was a wolf." Ferdinand is not seen again until the last scene, when he charges in on the Cardinal and Bosola, and stabs them both. Bosola stabs him in return, and just before Ferdinand dies, he "seems to come to himself," saying, "Whether we fall by ambition, blood, or lust, / Like diamonds, we are cut with our own dust."

Julia

Julia is the wife of an old nobleman and is the Cardinal's mistress. While she is staying with the Cardinal, she is propositioned by Delio, whom she refuses; she also tries to seduce Bosola. Ironically, the Cardinal kills her by tricking her into kissing a poisoned book, while she is swearing to keep his secret.

Fate and Belief

Considering that one of the main characters of *The Duchess of Malfi* is a Cardinal, one of the highest-ranking officials in the Roman Catholic Church, there is a surprising lack of reference to God in the play. The characters do not turn to God for help in trouble, and they do not seek forgiveness when they come to believe they have acted wrongly. The only certainty in life is death, and there is no promise here of an afterlife. The world of *The Duchess of Malfi* is controlled not by God, but by fate.

Ferdinand is the character most conscious of his religion, but his Christianity is not a religion of love but one of vengeance, not of forgiveness but of damnation. In act 2, in his anger at learning of the Duchess's child, Ferdinand's first instinct is to call her "a sister damn'd." Naming wild punishments he would like to administer to her, he declares that he would like to have the Duchess and the unknown father of the child "burnt in a coal-pit" with no vents, so that "their curs'd smoke might not ascend to heaven." In act 4, he brings a series of horrors to the Duchess to drive her to despair, so that she will renounce God and be sent to hell when he has her murdered. Ferdinand is so clearly insane, that his understanding of religion must be seen as a product of rage, not of religious teaching.

Other characters turn elsewhere for their understanding of the world. Antonio learns by astrological calculation that his first child will have a "short life" and a "violent death." The Cardinal, whose lavish lifestyle and mistress would seem to distance him from the teachings of his church, does not suggest that the Duchess pray for guidance if she finds herself tempted to remarry, but advises that "your own discretion / Must now be your director." Cariola warns the Duchess not to use a false religious pilgrimage to fool her brothers, but the Duchess rejects the warning, calling Cariola "a superstitious fool." Although she faces her death on her knees to more easily pass through heaven's gates, there is no real sense of faith in her last speeches.

Of all the characters, it is Bosola who most changes during the play, and whose psychology is revealed the most clearly. As he watches the conduct of the three siblings, he comes to a new understanding of the differences between a good servant and a good man, and he grows in respect for the honesty of Antonio and the dignity of the Duchess. If anyone were going to turn to God in the end, it would be Bosola, but he does not. Instead, when he realizes that he has accidentally killed Antonio, he utters the line that expresses the world view for the entire play: "We are merely the stars' tennis-balls, struck and banded / Which way please them."

Appearances and Reality

Repeated throughout *The Duchess of Malfi* is the idea that people cannot be trusted, that things are not as they appear. People, both the essentially good people and the villains, disguise their bodies and their motives. In act 1, several instances of pretending and concealing occur to set the tone for the rest of the play: the Cardinal pretends to have no interest in Bosola; Bosola is hired to spy on the Duchess, pretending only to tend her horses; the Duchess pretends to have no interest in marriage; Cariola hides behind the arras without Antonio's knowledge and promises the Duchess that she will "conceal this secret from the world *As warily as those that trade in poison* Keep poison from their children." Antonio, who is known for his honesty, agrees to keep the marriage a secret. The Duchess complains that women of wealth and stature cannot be honest about their feelings, but are "forc'd to express our violent passions *In riddles, and in dreams, and leave the path* Of simple virtue, which was never made / To seem the thing it is not."

Topics for Further Study

- Research another influential Renaissance text, Machiavelli's *The Prince* (1517), which describes the qualities of the ideal ruler. To what extent is the Cardinal an embodiment of these qualities? What are the strengths and weaknesses of such a ruler?

- Some critics have said that in creating the Duchess of Malfi, Webster was praising Queen Elizabeth I, who had died in 1603, ten years before the play was written. In what ways were Elizabeth I and King James I different? Why might Webster have preferred a ruler like Elizabeth I?

- London's Globe Theatre, one of the

theaters where *The Duchess of Malfi* was performed, has been reconstructed with historical accuracy. Research the ways in which the type of theater, and the conventions about casting a play, would have made a performance of the play seen in London in 1613 different from performances staged in important theaters today.

- Compare the Duchess's situation at the beginning of the play with the social conventions observed by British nobility today. How free, for example, are members of the Royal Family to marry whomever they wish, regardless of class distinctions or other considerations? How much pressure might one's family exert over one's choice of a spouse?

- *The Duchess of Malfi* is set in sixteenth century Italy, but written for a seventeenth century English audience. Given the broadest outline of the Duchess's story, what adaptations would a playwright have to make to set the story in twenty-first-century United States? How might American cultural values change the outcome of the story?

Further incidents of deception and disguise occur throughout the play. The Duchess and Antonio invent stories to conceal the birth of their first child and their plans to escape to Ancona. Ferdinand brings the Duchess a dead man's hand that he knows she will take for Antonio's and shows her wax figures that look like her husband and children. Bosola visits the imprisoned Duchess in disguise, appearing as an old man and a bellman. Even Bosola's one kindness to the Duchess is a deception, as he tells the dying Duchess that her husband is alive and reconciled with her brothers. The Cardinal kills Julia (with whom he has been having an affair without her husband's knowledge) by giving her a poison disguised as a holy book, not knowing that Julia has deceived him by hiding Bosola behind the door. The Cardinal, Bosola, and Ferdinand die without anyone coming to save them, because the Cardinal has lied to keep the servants from entering his chambers.

Although none of these deceptions brings about its desired end, the characters turn again and again to secrecy and disguise to solve their problems, as though they know no other way to move in the world. It is not an optimistic picture, as Bosola realizes just before he dies: "O, this gloomy world! / In what a shadow, or deep pit of darkness, / Doth womanish and fearful mankind live!" If the world is steered not by God but by uncaring stars, and if men and women cannot trust their own perceptions to steer through it, it is a gloomy world, indeed.

Style

Revenge Tragedy

Between 1542 and 1642 in England, many dramatists looked back to early Latin writers for their models. In particular, one group of English Renaissance plays, later called Revenge Tragedies, was based on the tragedies written by the Roman philosopher and playwright Seneca, who lived from 4 B.C. to A.D. 65. Seneca's tragedies employed a set of conventional characters and plot devices that these Renaissance writers found appealing, and at the end of the sixteenth century, English plays imitating Seneca began to appear. William Shakespeare (1564–1616) wrote two plays, *Titus Andronicus* (c. 1590) and *Hamlet* (c. 1601) that are generally considered to be revenge tragedies. Although *The Duchess of Malfi* is often labeled a revenge tragedy, it is more accurate to say that it was strongly influenced by the movement, but that Webster uses revenge tragedy conventions to create a different kind of play.

The nine Senecan tragedies have several features in common: a five-act structure; a theme of revenge; long-suffering nobles; trustworthy female companions; ghosts; gruesome violence inspired by lust, incest, and vengeance; the death of children; and a chorus that comments on the action and describes the violent acts, which happen offstage.

During the Elizabethan period, playwrights began to present the violence on stage in response to demands from audiences, who were accustomed to public executions and other forms of public violence. To Seneca's ingredients, they added a hero who is called upon but unwilling to seek revenge, actual or feigned insanity, and an emphasis on schemes and secrets.

Clearly, many of these elements are present in *The Duchess of Malfi*, but it varies from the conventions in important ways. The revenge tragedy has a hero whose honor has been wronged (often it is a son avenging his father); in this play, the brothers seek revenge on the Duchess, who has done them no harm. The Duchess is surely the hero of the play named for her, and yet she does not seek or win vengeance for the harm done to her. The fact that she is killed in act 4 (and does not die in the act of winning revenge) deflects attention away from her as the center of the action and moves the play out of the category of revenge tragedy. The motive for the actions of the two brothers is unclear, but revenge— whatever they may think themselves—is not at the heart of it.

Blank Verse

Many of the lines spoken by the characters in *The Duchess of Malfi* are written in a poetic form called blank verse. Blank verse is the name given to unrhymed lines of ten syllables each, accented on the even-numbered syllables, though lines need not be in perfectly regular iambic pentameter (the name given to lines constructed in this way) for the poetry to be labeled blank verse. For example, Ferdinand at one point wishes he were a wild storm "That I might toss her palace 'bout her ears, / Root up her goodly forests, blast her meads." Each of these lines has exactly ten syllables, and the underlying pulse or stress felt as one reads the lines naturally gives a slight accent on the second, fourth, sixth, eighth, and tenth syllables of each line. If every line were so regular, however, the speeches would develop a singsong rhythm that would be unnatural and distracting, so the poet's task is to write lines that are near enough to the regular pattern but with enough variety that different characters speak differently, and different tones can be heard. In fact, very few lines in *The Duchess of Malfi* are regular ten-syllable lines; most have more or fewer syllables or stresses in different places, as in the line "We are merely the stars' tennis-balls, struck and banded."

Not all of the lines in *The Duchess of Malfi* are written in verse. Antonio speaks in prose with Bosola and with Ferdinand before Antonio marries the Duchess, and the eight madmen speak in prose. The Duchess and Bosola speak in prose while he is disguised as the tomb-maker, but they shift to verse when he declares his intention to kill her. The blank verse is thought to convey solemnity and nobility, and all of the important speeches by important people are in blank verse. (An interesting use of this idea is Shakespeare's *Henry IV, Part I*, in which Prince Hal speaks in prose when he is with his friends in the tavern and speaks in blank verse when he is with the King or on the battlefield.)

Using blank verse for tragedy was a convention for Elizabethan dramatists. The first English tragedy, *Gorboduc* (1561), was also the first English drama written in blank verse, in a deliberate attempt to echo in English the regular rhythms of Senecan tragedy, written in Latin. Christopher Marlowe and William Shakespeare brought the form to its greatest heights with their writing some thirty or forty years later. A generation after these two, Webster and his contemporaries were still writing tragedies in blank verse, though never as well.

Webster frequently ends a scene with two rhyming lines, called a couplet. The rhyme catches the audience's ear, making the last lines of a scene slightly more noticeable and giving a finished quality, rather like a period at the end of a sentence. Within fifty years after the publication of *The Duchess of Malfi*, most English poetic drama was written entirely in couplets.

The Renaissance

The term "Renaissance" means "rebirth," and the period known as the Renaissance was a time of new beginnings in Europe, an emergence from the Middle Ages. The Renaissance brought with it new ways of thinking about science, religion, philosophy, and art. During the earlier medieval period, Europeans had come to think of themselves as insignificant creatures subject to and inferior to divine beings. When some Italian scholars began to read ancient Latin and Greek texts that had been ignored for centuries, they began to look for ways to combine contemporary Christian thought with the classical belief in human capabilities. This belief in what is now called Renaissance humanism drove a new passion for celebrating human endeavor and potential. The ideal "Renaissance man" would be talented in science, mathematics, poetry, art, and athletics.

As an intellectual movement, the Renaissance touched every aspect of life. Science and exploration proliferated. Political theorists attempted to apply the best features of classical thought, and religious reformers asserted the rights of the common person to have direct access to Biblical texts. There was a new passion for reading classical literature in the original Greek and Latin and for incorporating classical mythology into literature and art. New forms emerged, based on classical forms, as the revenge tragedy grew out of the study of Senecan tragedy. Literature, including drama, moved beyond its role as an outgrowth of the church and turned to stories that celebrated or decried human capabilities.

Of course, there was no particular day on which the Middle Ages ended and the Renaissance began. The transformation happened over many years and did not affect every country at the same time. Generally, the Renaissance is said to have begun in Italy during the fourteenth century and to have reached England about a century later. The height of the English Renaissance was during the sixteenth century and the beginning of the seventeenth. Webster's career comes at the end of this period, and *The Duchess of Malfi* shows many traces of its creation during this period. The Duchess's insistence that she be allowed to make individual choices, the secular tone of the play, the five-act structure and blank verse, the allusions to classical mythology, and the Cardinal's many references to new technology and science all point to the play as coming from the Renaissance.

One aspect of Renaissance literature that may strike readers in the twenty-first century as peculiar is the notion of imitation. Greek and Roman students frequently copied from models to create their own compositions, and the Renaissance writers adopted this technique. The basic story of the Duchess of Malfi, for example, is a true story that occurred in Italy around 1510. The story was adapted in Italian in a sixteenth-century novella, and in English in William Painter's collection of stories, *The Palace of Pleasure* and Sir Philip Sidney's *Arcadia*, Webster used incidents from all of these sources—sometimes using lines and phrases word for word—in creating his own play. He also kept a journal throughout his career, jotting down scraps of poetry and quotations he found interesting. He drew freely from this journal in writing his plays, inserting lines where they fit pleasingly. This was not considered plagiarism but a sensible way to draw on the learning of those who had come before.

Jacobean Age

The period within the Renaissance when England was ruled by King James I is known as the Jacobean period, from the Latin form of the name James. James I ruled from the death of Elizabeth I in 1603 until his own death in 1625, and although he was not a beloved king, the years of his reign saw a great period of English drama. William Shakespeare, for example, began his career before James came to the throne, but his greatest and most mature work was produced during the Jacobean age. Webster also produced his best work during these years, as did many other important dramatists.

Compare & Contrast

- **Early Seventeenth Century:** King

James I is ruler of England and Scotland. He has come to the throne through inheritance and divine right and is the sole ruler of the country.

Today: Queen Elizabeth II is Queen of England. She inherited the throne from her father, but her duties are primarily ceremonial. The country is ruled by a Parliamentary government.

- **Early Seventeenth Century:** The mental illness called melancholia is thought to be caused by an excess of black bile in the body. Some people deliberately take on the characteristics of melancholia, because it is thought to be a disease that affects great minds. Bosola may be one of these.

  Today: Depression is a widespread disorder, thought to be caused by a chemical imbalance. In technologically advanced countries, antidepressant medications are widely used.

- **Early Seventeenth Century:** Most noble women do not marry for love. Like the Duchess, they may be joined in arranged marriages with older men while they are very young. Even if widowed, they are not free to remarry or to make choices about their property without male guidance.

Today: While social pressures may prevent members of the upper classes from marrying those of the lower classes, there are no legal divisions between the classes. English women may marry whomever they wish and control their own property.

- **Early Seventeenth Century:** All that is required for a marriage to be legally binding in England is that a man and woman declare themselves to be husband and wife. Witnesses and written documents are not required.
  Today: Marriages must be performed by an official certified by the state to do so.

James's rule was guided by the strength of his religious convictions. He was a member of the Church of England, and it was under his direction that the King James Bible was produced. James also believed devoutly in the divine right of kings, or the idea that kings and queens are accountable only to God, and that the system of inheriting the monarchy was created by God. Because the Church of England was the official religion of the monarch and of the country, religion and politics were intertwined in a way that is not the same in England today. The divine right of kings gave James power, while the Roman Catholic idea of a pope chosen by God opposed that power. To protect his stature, James dealt severely with those who believed differently, including Puritans (who eventually began to leave England for the New World), Catholics (who are portrayed with irreverence in Webster's character of the Cardinal), and Jews (who are treated with casual disrespect in *The Duchess of Malfi* and other popular works of literature from the period).

Critical Overview

The Duchess of Malfi is considered one of Webster's two greatest works and one of the canonical works of Jacobean drama. It is also roundly criticized as being weak, confusing, and illogical. In his thorough overview of more than three centuries of criticism, *John Webster and His Critics 1617–1964*, Don D. Moore writes that there may be no one other than Webster "whose plays have received a more varied reception and whose critics have been so divided among themselves on whether the writer was due praise or excoriation." In Webster's own time, *The Duchess of Malfi* sold enough tickets to be profitable, and the publication of the play in 1623 was accompanied by verses from other playwrights who seem to have found the play worthy of praise.

From the second half of the seventeenth century through the eighteenth, the play was seldom performed and there was no extended criticism of it. Criticism of the nineteenth century tended more toward appreciation than study, and Webster was alternately praised for his overall effect or reviled for specific flaws in logic or ideology. Much of this criticism was based on performances, rather than on scrutiny of the text. Academic criticism, beginning in the late nineteenth century, focused at first on uncovering the sources for Webster's understanding of the Duchess's story.

In the twentieth century, dozens of critics have written about the play. William Archer, writing a 1920 article for *Nineteenth Century*, is typical of those who have found the play lacking. Inspired to examine the play closely after seeing a production, Archer found it "three hours of coarse and sanguinary melodrama" and pronounced it "fundamentally bad." With unblinking honesty, Archer points out several bits of inconsistency and illogic in the play, including the son of the Duchess and her first husband, who is mentioned only once in the play and then forgotten. Inga-Stina Ekeblad, on the other hand, explains in an article in *Review of English Studies* that Webster, "though he often leaves us in confusion," does achieve in this play a fusion of convention and realism, "creating something structurally new and vital."

Psychological questions about the play have been raised by several critics. What is Ferdinand's motive for tormenting his sister? Sheryl Craig believes that the answer lies in the fact that the Duchess and Ferdinand are twins. She explains in an article in *Publications of the Missouri Philological Association* that for Renaissance audiences, the siblings would have resembled biblical twins, whose "conflicts with each other are symbolic of their conflicts with God; one twin is the chosen one, God's elect, and the other twin is the outsider." Much more common is the opinion expressed by James Calderwood in *Essays in Criticism*, that within Ferdinand's actions are "unmistakable suggestions of incestuous jealousy." Calderwood finds that when Ferdinand becomes aware of his own sinful desires, he becomes a "physician-priest-executioner who seeks the purgation of his own tainted blood in the purging of hers."

Another central question that has engaged critics grows out of that fact that the title character dies in act 4. Is the Duchess really the main character of the play and, if so, what is the play about? Charles Hallett and Elaine Hallett, in *The Revenger's Madness: A Study of Revenge Tragedy Motifs*, write that the play is a drama of initiation, much like *Hamlet*, and that the Duchess is at the heart of it: "The test she must pass is whether she will remain the woman she was, once she sees what the world is." Kimberly Turner examines the play as a critique of the female ruler within the context of Renaissance patriarchy in an article in the *Ben Jonson Journal*, and finds that Webster creates a new kind of female hero who "participates actively in her own life."

What Do I Read Next?

- *The White Devil*, published in 1612, is Webster's other well-known play. Like *The Duchess of Malfi*, it is based on a true story of Italian nobles. Using elements of the revenge tragedy, it depicts diabolical brothers punishing and avenging their sisters.

- William Shakespeare's great tragedy *Hamlet, Prince of Denmark* (c. 1601) is arguably his most famous play. Although it ends, like *The Duchess of Malfi*, with dead bodies strewn across the stage, its focus is on the philosophical and psychological development of the title character.

- *Titus Andronicus* (c. 1590), another Shakespeare play, more closely resembles *The Duchess of Malfi* in its horrific violence. Seldom performed, it has a cycle of vengeance that includes murder, rape, the cutting off of a character's tongue and hands, and the baking of murdered children into a pie that is served to their mother.

- A good introduction to the period in which *The Duchess of Malfi* is set is

J. H. Plumb's *The Italian Renaissance*, published in a revised edition in 2001. The first half of the book is an historical overview of the economic and social conditions that led to the Renaissance; the second half includes brief biographies of important figures by different scholars.

Sources

Archer, William, "*The Duchess of Malfi*," in *Twentieth Century Interpretations of "The Duchess of Malfi*," edited by Norman Rabkin, Prentice-Hall, 1968, p. 14, originally published in *Nineteenth Century*, Vol. 87, 1920, pp. 126–32.

Calderwood, James L., "*The Duchess of Malfi*: Styles of Ceremony," in *Twentieth Century Interpretations of "The Duchess of Malfi*," edited by Norman Rabkin, Prentice-Hall, 1968, pp. 79, 82, originally published in *Essays in Criticism*, Vol. 12, 1962, pp. 133–47.

Craig, Sheryl, "'She and I were twins': Double Identity in *The Duchess of Malfi*," in *Publications of the Missouri Philological Association*, Vol. 19, 1994, p. 21.

Ekeblad, Inga-Stina, "The 'Impure Art' of John Webster," in *Twentieth Century Interpretations of "The Duchess of Malfi*," edited by Norman Rabkin, Prentice-Hall, 1968, p. 50, originally published in *Review of English Studies*, Vol. 9, 1958, pp. 253–67.

Hallett, Charles A., and Elaine S. Hallett, *The Revenger's Madness: A Study of Revenge Tragedy Motifs*, University of Nebraska Press, 1980, p. 286.

Moore, Don D., *John Webster and His Critics 1617–1964*, Louisiana State University Press, 1966, p. ix.

Turner, Kimberly A., "The Complexity of Webster's Duchess," in the *Ben Jonson Journal*, Vol. 7, 2000, p. 400.

Further Reading

Bloom, Harold, ed., *Elizabethan Dramatists*, Modern Critical Views series, Chelsea House, 1986.

> This collection of critical essays includes two essays about *The Duchess of Malfi* as well as essays about Webster's most important contemporaries. In "Tragical Satire in *The Duchess of Malfi*," Alvin B. Kernan describes Bosola as the ideal, and one of the last, of the Elizabethan satirists. G. Wilson Knight contributes an essay called simply "*The Duchess of Malfi*," which examines image clusters in the play.

Boklund, Gunnar, *"The Duchess of Malfi": Sources, Themes, Characters*, Harvard University Press, 1962.

> Boklund traces Webster's sources for the story of the Duchess, pointing out the places where Webster deviates from these sources to make the story his own. The characterization of Antonio as humble but honest, for example, is Webster's invention.

Knight, G. Wilson, "*The Duchess of Malfi*," in

Elizabethan Dramatists, edited by Harold Bloom, Modern Critical Views series, Chelsea House, 1986, pp. 85–107.

> Knight offers a close reading of the clusters of images and symbols in the play and argues that the coherence of the play is not to be found in the logical structure of the plot but in the non-rational resonance of the imagery.

Rabkin, Norman, ed., *Twentieth Century Interpretations of "The Duchess of Malfi,"* Prentice-Hall, 1968.

> This collection touches on the major critical questions about the play in ten critical essays, or "Interpretations," and fourteen brief excerpts, or "View Points," by scholars including T. S. Eliot and Northrup Frye.

Thomson, Leslie, "Fortune and Virtue in *The Duchess of Malfi,*" in *Comparative Drama*, Vol. 33, No. 4, 1999–2000, pp. 474–94.

> Thomson compares the play with medieval and Renaissance iconography illustrating the relationships between fortune, love, and death. She shows how the relationships between the Duchess (fortune) and Antonio (love) are derived from earlier morality plays

and emblem books.

Winston, Mathew, "Gendered Nostalgia in *The Duchess of Malfi*," in *The Renaissance Papers*, 1998, pp. 103–13.

> Winston sees in the play the longing of Webster and his contemporaries for Queen Elizabeth I, who had been dead for a decade when *The Duchess of Malfi* was first performed. The Duchess's death in act 4 is part of Webster's overall plan, which is to show in act 5 how the world decays when she is gone.

Lightning Source UK Ltd.
Milton Keynes UK
UKHW022338281220
375969UK00007B/377